The Russian Americans

RICHARD A. BOWEN

MAJOR AMERICAN IMMIGRATION

MASON CREST PUBLISHERS • PHILADELPHIA

Ornate spires rise above
Catherine Palace in
Pushkin, Russia.

The Russian Americans

RICHARD A. BOWEN

MAJOR AMERICAN IMMIGRATION

MASON CREST PUBLISHERS • PHILADELPHIA

Mason Crest Publishers
370 Reed Road
Broomall PA 19008
www.masoncrest.com

First printing

1 3 5 7 9 8 6 4 2

Library of Congress Cataloging-in-Publication Data

Bowen, Richard A.
  The Russian Americans / Richard A. Bowen.
      p. cm. — (Major American immigration)
  Includes index.
  ISBN 978-1-4222-0617-1
  ISBN 978-1-4222-0684-3 (pbk.)
  1. Russian Americans—Juvenile literature. 2. Russian Americans—
History—Juvenile literature. 3. Immigrants—United States—
History—Juvenile literature. 4. United States—Ethnic relations—
Juvenile literature. I. Title.
  E184.R9M67 2008
  973'.049171—dc22
                                                    2008026017

Table of Contents

MAJOR AMERICAN IMMIGRATION

America's Ethnic Heritage

Barry Moreno, librarian

Statue of Liberty/

Ellis Island National Monument

Ethnic diversity is one of the most striking characteristics of the American identity. In the United States the Bureau of the Census officially recognizes 122 different ethnic groups. North America's population had grown by leaps and bounds, starting with the American Indian tribes and nations—the continent's original people—and increasing with the arrival of the European colonial migrants who came to these shores during the 16th and 17th centuries. Since then, millions of immigrants have come to America from every corner of the world.

But the passage of generations and the great distance of America from the "Old World"—Europe, Africa, and Asia—has in some cases separated immigrant peoples from their roots. The struggle to succeed in America made it easy to forget past traditions. Further, the American spirit of freedom, individualism, and equality gave Americans a perspective quite different from the view of life shared by residents of the Old World.

Immigrants of the 19th and 20th centuries recognized this at once. Many tried to "Americanize" themselves by tossing away their peasant clothes and dressing American-style even before reaching their new homes in the cities or the countryside of America. It was not so easy to become part of America's culture, however. For many immigrants, learning English was quite a hurdle. In fact, most older immigrants clung to the old ways, preferring to speak their native languages and follow their familiar customs and traditions. This was easy to do when ethnic neighborhoods abounded in large North American cities like New York, Montreal, Philadelphia, Chicago, Toronto, Boston, Cleveland, St. Louis, New Orleans and San Francisco. In rural areas, farm families—many of them Scandinavian, German, or Czech—established their own tightly knit communities. Thus foreign languages and dialects, religious beliefs, Old World customs, and certain class distinctions flourished.

The most striking changes occurred among the children of immigrants, whose hopes and dreams were different from those of their parents. They began breaking away from the Old World customs, perhaps as a reaction to the embarrassment of being labeled "foreigner." They badly wanted to be Americans, and assimilated more easily than their parents and grandparents. They learned to speak English without a foreign accent, to dress and act like other Americans. The assimilation of the children of immigrants was encouraged by social contact—games, schools, jobs, and military service—which further broke down the barriers between immigrant groups and hastened the process of Americanization. Along the way, many family traditions were lost or abandoned.

Today, the pride that Americans have in their ethnic roots is one of the abiding strengths of both the United States and Canada. It shows that the theory which called America a "melting pot" of the world's people was never really true. The thought that a single "American" would emerge from the combination of these peoples has never happened, for Americans have grown more reluctant than ever before to forget the struggles of their ethnic forefathers. The growth of cultural studies and genealogical research indicates that Americans are anxious not to entirely lose this identity, whether it is English, French, Chinese, African, Mexican, or some other group. There is an interest in tracing back the family line as far as records or memory will take them. In a sense, this has made Americans a divided people; proud to be Americans, but proud also of their ethnic roots.

As a result, many Americans have welcomed a new identity, that of the hyphenated American. This unique description has grown in usage over the years and continues to grow as more Americans recognize the importance of family heritage. In the end, this is an appreciation of America's great cultural heritage and its richness of its variety.

P & O Pencilling

A passenger ship of the Peninsular & Oriental Steam Navigation Company is moored off the Isle of Wight in this illustration. Russian immigrants often had to travel to England before they could board a ship to the United States.

1 The Story of Sylvia Broter

Sylvia Broter was born near the wheat fields of a tiny Russian village. Her birth records are unclear, but her father registered her birth date for school as August 14, 1911. All the Jewish people lived in the town where Sylvia was born. The Christian people lived outside the town as farmers. Sylvia's father was Jewish and educated. He worked for a wheat farmer as a bookkeeper. He came to the United States in 1914 because of the Russian **pogroms** and because he wanted his freedom and the chance to raise his family in a better place.

Sylvia's father spoke no English. When officials asked him his name when he arrived at Ellis Island in New York Harbor, he did not understand the question. Because he was standing next to a woman who was also a passenger on the ship, they asked her, "Is this your brother?" Sylvia's father nodded, and they wrote down "Brother" as his name. Through the years, the H was dropped and his name became Broter. When he became a citizen, he could have changed it back to the family name, but he kept the name the way it was. "It's much easier to spell Broter than Zamarchovsky," he explained. So Sylvia's last name became Broter as well.

Sylvia's father arrived in the United States on the last ship before ocean travel was cut off because of World War I. The factories were thriving because of the war, so he got a job and was able to build a home in Toledo, Ohio.

When the rest of the family arrived in 1922, however, Sylvia's father became a peddler. He sold clothing out of the back of a wagon. He could no longer work in the factory because he had gotten sick with tuberculosis (TB), which was a common lung disease at the time. Although he was cured, he was told not to work indoors anymore.

Sylvia and her mother could not get a *visa* to get out of Russia. They had to sneak across the border to Poland, ending up in a house where they could safely rest before making the rest of their journey. Their next stop was Warsaw, the capital city of Poland. It was the first time they had seen a big city besides Kamenitz. It was beautiful.

They waited for their visa for nine months. In Warsaw they stayed with cousins whose last name was Silverman. Mr. and Mrs. Silverman had a son and a daughter. The father operated a shop where he sold dolls, little toy animals, and decorations. "Everyone was poor," Sylvia remembers, "but nobody felt poverty. We were all the same." Sylvia, her mother, and the Silvermans never lacked anything. Everyone always had enough food and clothing to survive.

The visas were finally granted. They were for Holland, so Sylvia and her mother traveled there. When they arrived, they boarded a ship bound for the United States. The boat was rocking in the huge waves. They had to travel in a cabin in the lower part of the ship, where they slept on bunk beds—one for Sylvia and one for her mother. They would go up on the deck occasionally to see the ship rolling in the water, but spent most of their time in the cabin. The trip was supposed to take two weeks, but it took three weeks because of a storm.

A Russian peddler poses with his goods. Peddlers traveled from town to town, and often had to rely on residents for shelter and food.

Women pause to socialize during a day of farm work in Russia. The practice of serfdom originated in 1598 when Boris Godunov, the ruler of Russia, decreed that peasants could not leave the land where they had been born. This law forced Russian peasants to work the land for wealthy landowners almost as though they were slaves. By the mid-19th century, Russian census figures reported that of the country's 62 million people, more than 23 million (37 percent) were serfs. The laws regarding serfs were abolished in 1861.

When they got to the United States, they had to stop at Ellis Island, where doctors examined them to see if they met the health requirements. They were standing next to a couple from Holland. The woman's thumb was black from an infection or a fungus. The doctors consulted with one another and decided that the woman had to return home. The couple was denied entry into the United States; they had to get back on the ship and return to Holland.

Sylvia and her mother were in a big room sitting on a bench waiting with a large group of people. There they watched a black-and-white movie starring Charlie Chaplin. Sylvia was thrilled. This was the first movie she had ever seen. After the movie, while she continued to wait with the other people, a black gentleman walked by. Sylvia had never seen a person of color before, either, and didn't know what to think. Her mother didn't either, but they both kept quiet because everything was so different and they didn't want to ask too many questions.

> Sylvia remembers a pogrom that occurred in Russia when she was a small girl. She recalls someone yelling, "Oh, my goodness, the soldiers are coming!" One of her family members grabbed her and put her down in the cellar. "It was completely black," Sylvia remembered. Her mother said, "Don't be afraid. God is with you." Sylvia was unharmed and recalls, "Even to this day, I don't have fear; I always feel that with God, you don't have to be afraid."

No one met them at Ellis Island. They were to go on to Toledo, Ohio, but they didn't have enough money for the train. A check was supposed to have been waiting for them, but it wasn't there. They sent a telegram and waited, sleeping on a bench overnight. Sylvia wasn't afraid because she was with her mother. As long as they were together, it was like a big adventure. Finally, the money came.

Sylvia's father met them at the train when they arrived in Toledo. Sylvia was disappointed because she expected a strong man with dark curly hair. Instead, her father was bald and a little stooped over. Her father and mother had a happy reunion: they kissed and hugged each other when they met. Together, the family traveled to their lovely new home. It was a two-family house with two rose bushes, a lilac bush, an apple tree, and a walnut tree in the backyard.

A couple of years later, Sylvia's sister was born. Each of the girls had their own bedroom until times grew hard during the Great Depression, which began in 1929. Then the family had to rent out part of the house, so the two girls slept in the living room. Sylvia said, "Fortunately, the FHA (Federal Housing Administration) let us keep the house, so we didn't lose it, thank goodness."

After the regular school day was done, there was a special class for *immigrants*. There were only three people in the class: two little Chinese boys and Sylvia. Nobody knew English; they were given short readings so they could learn. They felt different from the rest of their classmates. Sylvia said, "I would want to show off that I knew something, so I'd go to the blackboard and write down some

Immigrants arrive at Ellis Island, circa 1915. The migration of Russians to America between 1880 and 1920 intensified Russia's problems, as doctors, engineers, and scientists fleeing from Russia left the country with fewer and fewer educated citizens.

One program at Sylvia's school was for posture. With a special camera, a teacher took a silhouette picture of the students (a black picture against a white background). Then she rated their postures, from A to D. If she gave you a B, you were all right. Nobody had perfect posture. Sylvia was a C. Then the teacher instructed the children to do certain exercises that would help them improve. Later, the woman returned and took silhouettes again. Many of the students, including Sylvia, came out with an A. "We knew how to stand up straight and take care of ourselves, so this was a big boost. Not only did it assimilate me into American culture, but it gave me great confidence," Sylvia recalls.

of my math. But it was kind of a lost time in some ways, because they [the teachers] weren't doing that much for us, and it was okay. There was nothing else they could do."

The school officials put Sylvia in second grade, although she was 10 years old. She said, "My clothes were rather old-fashioned. My dresses were a little too long. So I had for a long time an *inferiority complex*." But she studied hard, began to get better grades, and learned as much English as she could.

During the 1920s, tuberculosis continued to be a common disease. When she arrived in the United States, Sylvia was a rosy-cheeked girl. When she began to look pale, her mother took her to see the doctor. He recommended that she go to a hospital in the country. It was a hospital where children went if they were in danger of getting tuberculosis. Sylvia lived at the hospital for 15 months. There, they had many classic books for young people, such as *Five Little Peppers and How They Grew*, and *The Secret Garden*. They were also served three meals a day, saw a movie once a week, and had ice cream after lunch on Wednesdays. When Sylvia was well and it was time to go home, she wanted to stay longer, because she was having such a good time.

Sylvia took grades four and five in one year, so when she returned to her regular public school, she had caught up to other students her age. She was in the sixth grade.

When she was in high school, a new store called the McCrory Five-and-Ten opened in Toledo. Sylvia got a summer job where she made $10 for working 48 hours a week. When it was time to return to school in the fall, she continued to work at the store in order to help her mother and father rather than going back to high school. Then she enrolled in night school to learn typing and shorthand. Because she wanted to work in an office as her career, she accepted little jobs in offices. She soon found out she was overworked and underpaid. Sylvia began to change jobs frequently, but she always gave two weeks' notice and remembered to get a recommendation. Sylvia says, "I did not 'burn bridges.' I always had a recommendation. But I made a mistake by quitting high school." Later, she got an excellent job at Bender Corporation and worked there for 20 years, until she retired.

Sylvia's story is fairly typical of many Russian Americans. She was part of a great wave of immigrants who came to the United States and Canada during the late 19th and early 20th century, hoping to start a new life in America. ✳

2 Why the Russians Came

In Russia, as well as in other parts of Europe, people began leaving their homelands for North America for a variety of reasons. These included political *oppression* and a desire for a better way of life. The two major factors for most of Europe were increased population and industrialization.

In Russia, some other factors were also involved. In 1547, *czar* Ivan the Terrible declared that all the peasants in the land were to become serfs. A *serf* farmed the land and gave nearly all he or she produced to the nobility. Serfs were considered property. When a landowner sold his land, the serfs were sold along with it. The only difference between a serf and a slave was that a serf was able to do what he or she wanted to do with their free time and could own some property. Rules were enforced by the czar's secret police. Anyone who did not like the rules was subject to imprisonment or death.

Ivan IV (known as "Ivan the Terrible" or "Ivan the Fearsome") became the first czar of Russia in 1547. During his rule, he helped to change Russia from a small state into a growing empire. Ivan passed laws restricting the mobility of Russia's peasants.

Czar Alexander II was known as "the Liberator" because he freed the serfs in 1861. He gained the throne after his father's death in 1855. Alexander attempted to reform Russian society during his rule. He was assassinated while driving in his carriage in 1881.

In Europe, many people were moving to newly industrialized cities because of the opportunity to get a job. In 1861, Czar Alexander II, who was in favor of a more modern type of government, gave Russia's serfs their freedom. At the same time the village councils, which were controlled by the nobility, adopted a land rotation policy. The policy said that the former serfs could not own the land on which they grew their food; they could only farm it for a little while. After that, the council gave it to someone else. Shortly thereafter, the councils reduced the amount of land the peasants farmed by one-half. These policies made it very difficult for them to survive. Consequently, many people were forced to leave the land they loved and move to the cities, where they had to work in factories.

Factory work made it no easier for families to live than farming had. Conditions were terrible. Most people had to work 12 hours a day, seven days a week. Average pay was 20 rubles a month. With this, a family could just barely buy the food they needed and pay the rent for a one-room apartment, which they often shared with another family.

The major European cities were becoming more industrialized. This meant more and more citizens stopped living a life centered on farming. Instead of living primarily by food, clothing, and shelter produced from the land, people got jobs in the cities. From the money they earned on the job, they purchased their necessities.

In the centuries before the 1870s, emigration out of *autocratic* Russia was forbidden. Peasants were not allowed to travel outside their own villages, much less to other lands. Thus, there were no large numbers of Russians leaving their country for North America. Later, emigration was no longer forbidden, but doing so was hard because it required money for travel and a visa, which was difficult to obtain. However, political and economic pressures forced some people to try to leave the country anyway.

In Russia, thousands of Jews were forced to leave because of violent, government-sponsored massacres called pogroms. Pogroms occurred in

Fannie Kligerman lived east of Kishinev, near Kiev, in a small but comfortable house with her family. She remembers, "We weren't poor, but we weren't rich. We always had food on the table." One summer day they found out the pogromers were coming to murder them and take their farm. Her father buried all of their knives and even the scissors so they could not be used for killing. A family friend who was a lawyer thought of an idea. He said, "Set up tables outside and put out plenty of whiskey." The pogromers came with their sacks to loot the house and their weapons to kill the people, but after they drank the whiskey, they were so drunk they forgot all about killing and looting. They left without hurting anyone.

many parts of European Russia, but they were especially vicious around a region called the *Pale*. This was an area of land located between the Baltic Sea and the Black Sea where Russian Jews were forced to live. In the Pale, most Jews were not allowed to reside in a city. Those who were paid dearly for the privilege. For instance, they could not own land and they had to work at certain jobs. The pogroms began in the 1880s. During one of these violent rampages from 1903 through 1907, 50,000 Jews were killed in the southwestern area of Russia near Kishinev. As a result, hundreds of thousands of Russian Jews looked to North America for freedom and safety.

The major *influx* of Russian immigrants came to North America during what is often called the "new" immigration. This occurred from

1890 through the early 1930s. (The "old" immigration involved only a few Russians and occurred from the early 1700s to the 1890s.) The world of the "new" immigrant was different from today's. There were few representative governments in which the people vote and elect the administration and where they had a voice in how their country operates. Instead, it was a world of kingdoms and autocrats, **tyranny** and brutality. Many people were suffering as a result of autocratic governments.

In Russia, the czar continued to rule the country. Similar to a king or an emperor, the czar had absolute power and made decisions based not on what was good for most people in Russia, but on what would bring power and wealth to himself, his family, and his friends. Anyone who opposed the czar was put in jail or killed. The czar's family was considered royalty, and power was passed along from generation to

While many people were forced to go to the cities to find work, some people were simply tired of being farmers. Sonya Kevar, who grew up in Yasinoc, remembers that her family had a farm with cattle, two horses, chickens, and turkeys. Her parents also cut trees for lumber, which they transported by river to the sawmill. Sonya recalls her mother saying in 1906 that she "didn't want to be a farm lady anymore." In 1906, Sonya's father left for the United States. He sent for the rest of the family five years later.

generation, usually from father to oldest son. The czar granted his friends and family members, who were called dukes, princes, and barons, the right to own land and rule sections of the country.

If you were born a member of the lower class, there was no opportunity to advance into a higher **stratum** of society. Destiny was predetermined. Many Russians felt frustrated because they could do nothing but work land they did not own and give nearly all of the results of their labors to the wealthy landowners. Those were the oppressive rules of society, and most of the people had to live by them.

In North America, there were no such rules. A person or a family could become prosperous by working hard, saving their earnings, and investing their money wisely. Even an immigrant who owned very little upon his or her arrival in North America could succeed. Long work hours, low pay, political persecution, and a variety of other reasons forced more and more eyes to turn toward North America where opportunities seemed more plentiful. To many people in Russia, Canada and the United States seemed like the Golden Land, where people could find freedom from oppression. From 1899 to 1924, more than 1.7 million people emigrated from Russia to the United States. Of this number, more than 75 percent were Russian Jews. Russians made up the second-largest immigrant group to arrive in America during this time period.

After the Russian Revolution in 1917, the **Communist** government, headed by Vladimir Lenin, offered the poor peasants freedoms they had not known before. Life in Russia appeared to be getting better.

Vladimir Ilyich Lenin led the revolution that brought the Communist party to power in Russia, an occurrence which has been called the most important political event of the 20th century. Lenin spent years studying the works of Karl Marx and the technique of revolution and building a following to support his vision.

The people who were threatened by this revolution were those in the upper class and some members of the middle class. This was because the revolutionary leaders were taking away their land and possessions. Many of these people fled to cities in Europe, especially Paris and Belgrade. About 40,000 came to the United States and Canada.

After Lenin died, Joseph Stalin came to power. During his rule, which lasted 25 years, all hopes of improving life for the peasants were destroyed. His policies forbade practicing most of the traditional cultural and religious aspects of peasant life. He established large

concentration camps where 30 million men and women worked as slaves in cold and bitterly desolate conditions. Most of them died in these camps. Between 1930 and 1944, only about 14,000 people were able to immigrate to Canada and the United States.

Joseph Stalin was considered one of the most ruthless dictators of modern times, but he did succeed in transforming the Soviet Union into a major world power. His real name was Iosif Vissarionovich Dzhugashvili; he took the name Stalin in 1912 from the Russian world *stal*, meaning "steel."

At the end of World War II, an estimated eight million refugees who had lost their homes during the war were roaming the countryside. The Soviet government allowed 35,000 to come to the United States.

For the next 40 years, between 1951 and 1991, when the **Cold War** was being fought between the United States and the Soviet Union, Russians were not officially allowed to come to North America. Two groups of people did manage to escape, however. Some Jews, who had been given visas to live in Israel instead went to North America. The others were scientists and artists. At the time, the Soviet government was trying to show the world that its society and way of life could produce great art and advances in science. So the government allowed many prominent scientists and artists to travel to conferences and performances in other countries. These people then took the opportunity to seek **asylum** in free countries, including Canada and the United States.

Most recently, many Russians have come to North America in search of a better life since the collapse of the Soviet Union in 1991. That year, immigration from the Soviet republics grew to nearly 57,000. Since then, immigration has remained high. In 2007, for example, more than 60,000 people from former Soviet republics became U.S. citizens, including 41,593 people from Russia. ✺

How They Came

During the largest migration, which consisted mostly of Russian Jews during the years 1890 to 1920, the father of the household was often the first to move to North America. After he arrived and began to work at a job, he sent money to the family back in Russia to be saved for their passage later. The first family members to join him were usually the oldest sons and daughters so they could also earn money. This meant more help in bringing the rest of the family to the New World. Along with money, they often sent steamship tickets.

Immigrants wait in line at Ellis Island to receive a thorough inspection from immigration officials. Immigrants were examined to ensure they were healthy and carried no contagious diseases.

Travelers could not take large items along with them to their new life. The family sold their house and gave away or sold their furniture and other household items, often to relatives who were staying behind. The items they did take were hand-embroidered clothing, down quilts to remind them of the warmth of home, food for the journey, and pictures of friends and relatives. They transported these belongings in cloth sacks or homemade suitcases. ***Emigrants*** carried their money in a bag tied around their neck, for they could not afford to lose it. Upon arrival in the United States, everyone had to have at least $25 to prove **self-sufficiency**.

The journey itself had three parts: travel to the port of departure, the journey over the ocean, and the trip to the final destination in the Northern Hemisphere.

Because many people were victims of **genocide** or political persecution, they could not get a visa and had to leave Russia in secret. Therefore, travel to the port often involved bribing the guards and running across the border to Poland or Prussia under the cover of darkness. Although this may sound exciting, many people were in danger of losing their lives. They

A Russian woman washes her family's clothes in a river close to her village in this colored photograph from the 19th century.

probably would not have succeeded were it not for helpers along the way. These were friends who assisted the travelers by hiding them in their houses, barns, or woods until darkness fell and they could safely run across the border and continue on their journey.

Unlike today, there were few roads and even fewer automobiles. Emigrants traveled on foot or by train to the port. Some people had to take a ferryboat to cross lakes and other bodies of water. When many family members traveled together, they sometimes hired a horse and cart to carry all of the baggage. Robbers who wanted to steal their money and other items of value also made this a dangerous part of the journey.

Marchers parade through a Russian street during the Revolution of 1917. In the fall of 1917 the Bolshevik Party, led by Vladimir Lenin, overthrew the government of Russia and seized power. The Bolsheviks emerged victorious after a civil war from 1918 to 1921. In 1922, Lenin and his followers established the Union of Soviet Socialist Republics (USSR).

Arriving at the port meant relief for many people. They no longer had to look over their shoulders and be constantly on the alert for robbers and border guards. It also meant that perhaps the most dangerous part of their journey was over and the actual journey to the New World was about to begin. To many, it was a signal that at last they were leaving behind their old life for a new life in the Golden Land of Opportunity.

Immigration was a big business, and many people made their living providing services to the immigrants. These included immigration agents; owners of private and government-run hotels at the ports; railroad, ferry boat, and steamship employees; border guards; health officials; customs agents; and people who sold food and other necessities to the emigrants along the way.

Some people arrived at the port cities with a steamship ticket already purchased. Others had to buy their tickets when they got there. Because of the difficulty traveling overland, the people going to North America had trouble knowing exactly when they were going to arrive at the port city. Therefore, some could sail soon after they bought their tickets. Most others had to wait days or even weeks before they could sail, however.

The law required that the steamship companies house and feed the travelers who were waiting to board their ships. The companies put passengers up in boarding houses run by "landsmen." The government owned some of these facilities; others were privately owned. One woman reported, "We went to this great big house, where we stayed two weeks waiting for the boat. Oh, the grand food! There were pickled herrings...good butter, [and] homemade bread that they were baking there. Boy, did I have a feast!" Another person painted a different picture: "We stayed in a large building, maybe 15, 20, 30 beds in one big room. When they say you come for breakfast at seven o'clock sharp...you were there by the door at seven o'clock sharp. Because if you got there at seven-thirty or eight o'clock, there might not be enough food for you. The food was different from what I was used to, mostly hard rolls, hard bread, sometimes a little soup, sometimes a small piece of meat, other times just vegetables. If there was an extra roll, I put it in my pocket and saved it for later."

Immigrants were examined for diseases, both before leaving the port city and upon arrival in North America. Shipping company officials asked them questions regarding their marital status, financial resources, political and religious ties, country of origin, and final destination. A "wrong" answer might mean that a person would be denied entrance into North America and would have to return home.

By law, shipping companies were required to examine, vaccinate, and disinfect passengers before they could board the ships. Although the companies obeyed the law, they usually did a poor job of it, their main objective being to sell tickets and collect money. As a result, many people who could have had their medical problems cured before coming to North America were sent home because they were found to be unacceptable. Many who had sold their homes and possessions, left their families, and sailed

Refugees from Russia stand on the deck of a ship during the Russian Revolution in 1917. The Russian Revolution was the culmination of a series of small revolutions that began in 1825. The Russian people rebelled several times against the ruling classes before the successful revolutions that brought Lenin to power.

thousands of miles across the ocean were bitterly disappointed to find out they had to go back home.

After examining the passengers and questioning them, shipping companies were also required to file a ship's manifest of their passengers. This was a list of their "cargo," and it included details about their passengers' countries of origin, destinations, political affiliations, medical conditions, marital status, and financial resources. The shipping companies often did a careless job of this, which sometimes caused problems and confusion when the immigrants landed in America.

Famous steamships like the *Olympic*, *Lusitania*, and *Rotterdam*, as well as smaller vessels whose names have long been forgotten, provided transportation across the vast Atlantic Ocean. Most carried both passengers and cargo. Passengers traveled first, second, or third class. Third class is also known as steerage because it is near the ship's gears, pulleys, and other devices that make up the equipment that steer the boat. Steerage is the farthest level below deck. A typical steerage compartment at the time was six or eight feet high, with two or three tiers of metal bunks on which the steerage passengers slept. These compartments had no windows and very little air circulation.

Men and women stayed in separate areas; children remained with their mothers. The toilet facilities were primitive and rarely cleaned. Mingled with the other smells from the hold of the ship, the air in steerage had a terrible odor. Foul odors, the constant throbbing of the engines, and the pounding of the waves put many third-class passengers into a state of semiconsciousness; they only came to their senses when they landed.

During the heaviest period of Russian immigration, between 1890 and the early 1920s, steerage fare cost between $10 and $15. Only a few immigrants had enough money to travel first or second class, which cost more, so most traveled third class. Some companies jammed up to 2,000 passengers into the steerage areas of their larger ships. They did not feed them much, and made large profits as a result. Many companies provided huge barrels of **herring** for the steerage passengers to eat. This fish was cheap and supposedly prevented seasickness.

Seasickness was a constant problem for the immigrants. Few had traveled on the water for any length of time, and most were not used to the constant motion caused by the rolling waves. One passenger said: "It was so rough! A lot of the time you just lay in your bed when you don't feel so good. You don't get up...because if you do, you get dizzy and then you get more sick, because the water was so rough."

With the waves pounding the ship, the awful odors, and the rough conditions, some people actually cried all the way from Europe to North America. Upon arrival, their eyes were so red and puffy from crying that the doctors thought they were suffering from an eye condition and should be sent home.

Companies advertised that emigrants could travel on their ships and arrive in North America in five or six days. They said people would travel on a big, new ocean liner like the *Kaiser Wilhelm II*, which provided a smooth, fast ride. Often, however, when emigrants arrived in the port city, they found they would be traveling instead on a small, old boat that was much less seaworthy. They also found the journey would take three or four weeks instead of five or six days.

Many children, however, managed to have a wonderful time despite the hardships. The children were less susceptible to seasickness and often cared for the adults who were ill. When they had free time, the children spent hours exploring every corner of the ship, running up on deck, eating, and playing games. As one woman who came to America as a child later explained, "That trip, oh, I enjoyed it! Oh God, how I enjoyed it! We came on a third class, way at the bottom. [Mother]...was sitting in the cabin alone...but not me, I was all over."

Before 1892, immigrants were "processed" (checked for medical, financial, and other conditions) at Castle Garden Immigration Station in New York Harbor. Castle Garden was eventually closed because it was too small to handle the many new immigrants from Russia and eastern Europe. A new facility was constructed at Ellis Island, where millions of immigrants entered the United States. When the boat arrived, the first- and second-class passengers were let off first in the harbor. Then the steerage passengers were transferred to a ferryboat that took them to Ellis Island. Being "cleared" at Ellis Island meant you could meet your relatives and begin the journey to your final destination.

Many of the Russian immigrants at this time went to live in the Midwest in the cities of Detroit and Chicago. Some lived as farmers in

The great majority of the Russian immigrants who came to the United States and Canada from 1899 to 1924 were Jews. They made up more than three-quarters of the total emigration from Russia during this time period.

Canada's Manitoba province or the western states of Kansas, Minnesota, North and South Dakota, and Nebraska. Others worked in factories in Baltimore, New York, and Philadelphia. Those who had to journey overland often traveled by boat from New York Harbor through the Great Lakes and to their final destinations by train.

Most Russian Jews settled in the big cities of Chicago, Philadelphia, and New York. For the many who settled in New York, it was a short trolley or subway ride from the New York dock to their new home on the Lower East Side of the city.

Many newcomers had to share an apartment with relatives before finding their own accommodations. When they did find their own place, they sometimes had to keep *lodgers*, often other immigrants, in order to pay the rent.

What They Did

Most Russian immigrants who came to North America during the late 1800s and early 1900s had little education and few skills, except perhaps farming. English was a foreign language to them. Therefore, they often had to take hard jobs in factories and mines. Unscrupulous owners would take advantage of this situation and give immigrants the lowest paying, most dangerous jobs. Work was often 12 hours a day. Miners were subject to cave-ins and had to breathe coal dust, which resulted in injuries and lung diseases. In the steel mills, they carried large bags of coal on their backs to feed the blast furnaces. Those who became farmers were perhaps better off, for at least they could breathe the fresh air in the country and do work they knew how to do.

Tailors work to turn out garments in the slum district of New York City around 1900. The term "sweatshop" was coined to describe the uncomfortable and unsafe working conditions immigrants worked in to make a meager living.

Those working in cities sometimes had to share an apartment with people they did not know. For example, one factory worker in New York shared his room with four others. A Pittsburgh family rented an apartment that had three rooms. They lived in one windowless room and rented out another to five boarders. Everyone used the third room as a combination laundry, kitchen, and living room. Miners sometimes had to live in shacks made of old lumber, tar paper, and tin cans.

Some Russian Jews who immigrated were skilled craftsmen, such as painters, carpenters, or printers. Others were peddlers or clerks. A few were professionals, like doctors or lawyers. Only a small number of Russian Jews took jobs in heavy industry. Many entered the garment industry. Some had been tailors before coming to the New World. Others were so-called "Columbus tailors": they learned the trade upon arrival. In the late 1890s and early 1900s, the garment industry was experiencing tremendous growth, first in men's, and later in women's clothing. Another reason many people wanted to be in the clothing business was that it did not require a lot of start-up money. After a short time, a person might be able to start his or her own business and become prosperous.

The process of making clothing is easy to break down into small tasks. A person did not need to know how to make an entire jacket, for instance. He or she would only need to know how to make a part, like a sleeve or a collar. It was easy to train the uneducated immigrants to learn a job in a short period of time.

A large place where clothing was made was called a **sweatshop.** It got its name from the terrible heat generated when many people were working in a small enclosed area, especially in summer. One person described viewing a sweatshop from an elevated train during the early

1900s: "Every open window of the big tenements [buildings]…gives you a glimpse of one of those shops as the train speeds by. Men and women, bending over their machines or ironing boards at the windows, half-naked….[It is like] an endless workroom where vast multitudes are forever laboring. Morning, noon, and night, it makes no difference; the scene is always the same."

After the Communist Revolution in Russia in 1917, a new type of immigrant appeared in North America. These were the upper- and middle-class members of the former Russian aristocracy who had had their wealth taken away by the Russian revolutionaries. With little or no money, they were also without skills because previously, the serfs had provided them with everything they needed. Now they had to provide for themselves. Although they had few talents, these immigrants had retained their social graces. They found work in the hospitality industry as maids, waiters, and doormen. Many professionals in the middle

David Dubinsky, a Russian Jew, formed the International Ladies Garment Workers' Union in 1900 to help Jewish laborers in North America. Besides assisting workers in obtaining fair wages and good working conditions, this organization operated summer camps and health centers, built and maintained low-cost apartments, and provided adult education courses and day care centers. The organization still exists today with a membership of 175,000 people.

Women inspect produce on a crowded street in the Lower East Side of New York City. Most immigrants settled in crowded and filthy tenement buildings because they could not afford better living quarters.

class, such as doctors, lawyers, and professors, also had to flee the revolution. When they arrived in North America, although many had to learn English, they found they could continue working in their chosen fields.

With the collapse of the Soviet Union in 1991, more Russian immigrants have come to North America. Many recent arrivals are professionals: engineers, doctors, accountants, and so on. In order to pursue their careers, they have had to obtain licenses that allow them to practice their professions in their adopted country. This means studying and taking exams in addition to learning English. Therefore, some are temporarily working at lower-paying jobs, such as taxi drivers or janitors, in order to pay the bills while they study. ✸

Russian settlers to the American West built Fort Ross near the Russian River north of San Francisco, California. They sold the fort to a Swedish immigrant named John A. Sutter in 1841, just eight years before the discovery of gold on the land would spark the California Gold Rush.

5 Where They Settled

The first Russians to live in North America had been sent as hunters to Alaska and parts of California. During the 1700s, hunters had eliminated almost all of the fur-bearing animals on the Siberian coast of Russia, so the czar sent two ships to search for new hunting opportunities. The first landed on the Aleutian Islands, which are off the coast of Alaska. The islands were teeming with game. Traders and hunters soon followed the navy men in order to hunt fox, seal, and sea otter. They established a Russian settlement on Kodiak Island in 1784, which eventually had about 40 buildings.

Later, 30 serfs came to farm on the Alaskan mainland near the capital of Russian-America called Sitka. However, Sitka was in the middle of the native Tlingit area. The Tlingit were not happy that the Russians were living there. A few years later, after obtaining firearms from traders from the United States, they attacked Sitka, killing or capturing the 600 inhabitants and destroying the town itself. In two years, a Russian warship arrived and drove off the Tlingit. The Russians established another town in the same location called New Archangel.

In 1812, Fort Ross was established near the Russian River north of San Francisco, California. Ninety-five Russians came from New Archangel to raise food for the Russian settlements in Alaska, where the growing season is too short for agriculture. The fort was sold in 1841, and all the inhabitants returned to New Archangel.

In 1867, Russia sold Alaska to the United States. At that time, there were 208 Russian women and 576 men living in 43 villages and towns. The U.S. Army helped keep order until around 1877. When the soldiers left, many of the people did not want to stay because the area was lawless and wild. Some went to Canada, some to California. Three hundred returned to Russia.

The Great Plains of the United States attracted many immigrants from the 1870s through 1920. This was because this area was accessible by rail and offered fertile, inexpensive land. The plains provinces of Canada—Manitoba, Alberta, and Saskatchewan—were not reachable by rail until around 1900. After this time, immigration to the Canadian provinces increased because of the newly completed railroads. The Canadian government was actively trying to *recruit* people to live there. The railroad companies also needed people to expand and maintain the railroads.

The *Mennonites* were German Russians who were excellent farmers. One of their religious beliefs was that their men should not fight wars. After living peacefully in Russia for about 100 years, the Russians tried to force them to join the Russian army. As a result, the Mennonites decided to find areas in Canada and the United States where they could live. They emigrated in the 1870s to pursue opportunities for farming and to live peacefully as before. Many

A small Russian Orthodox church built by a colony of 50 Russians still stands near Lakewood, New Jersey. The Russian Orthodox church was forced to cooperate with the authorities of the Soviet Union in order to function until the restructuring of Communism allowed open worship after 1990.

settled in the Manitoba province of Canada; others went to the west and midwest parts of the United States.

The United States declared war against Germany in 1917. At that time, there was a definite anti-German attitude on the part of other Americans, which made the Mennonites feel threatened. Some Americans felt the Mennonites were cowards because they did not want to go to war or preferred to work in non-combat areas of the military. Consequently, some joined their fellow Mennonites in Canada rather than remain in the United States. Although some Mennonite communities remain, many of their members eventually drifted away from their cultural and religious beliefs as a result of the pressure they felt.

Another group called the **Molokans** left Russia between 1906 and 1907. They fled because their fellow Russians were harassing them for their *pacifist* beliefs during the Russian-Japanese War of 1904. In order to try and preserve their traditional religion, diet, and language, 5,000 went to the Los Angeles area in the United States, where they established farms. During World War I, the Molokans, like the Mennonites, also felt persecuted for their beliefs. Eventually, they, too, lost touch with their previous way of life and the Molokan culture completely disappeared.

Most Russians who came during the great migrations of the 19th and 20th centuries settled in the northeastern cities of the United States, such as New York and Philadelphia. Others went to Chicago, Detroit, and Buffalo. Smaller communities were established in the more rural parts of the United States. The people named them after towns and cities back in Russia, for example, Moscow, Idaho, and Odessa, Texas.

According to the 2000 census, the total population of the United States is 281 million. Of these, more than 11 million claim Russian heritage. Often, however, Russian immigrants to the United States or Canada did not pass along the Russian language or traditions to their children. This was because of intense pressure on the children to have the same cultural values as their classmates. Only a few close-knit Russian-American communities exist today. In San Francisco, the Russian-American community numbers around 110,000 people, and there is a substantial community in Brighton Beach, New York. These areas have Russian stores, businesses, restaurants, and yearly Russian festivals.

Overall, Russian Americans are a successful group. One recent survey found that as a group they are among the highest-paid of the major ethnic groups. Many are skilled scientists, artists, and other professionals. While striving to maintain the traditions of good food, music, dress, art, and humor, the people who make up this unique section of the population have used their freedom to better themselves and their families, contributing substantially to the accomplishments and prosperity of the North American nations in which they live. ✹

Chronology

1547 Czar Ivan the Terrible declares all Russian peasants are to become serfs.

1784 The first permanent Russian settlement in North America is established on Kodiak Island in Alaska.

1799 The first governor of Russian Alaska is appointed.

1800 Sitka, the capital of Russian America, is established.

1802 The native Tlingit destroy Sitka.

1804 Russians rebuild the capital on site of Sitka and rename it New Archangel.

1812 Fort Ross is established near the Russian River in California.

1867 Russia sells Alaska to the United States.

1877 U.S. Army leaves Alaska.

1870 Mennonites from Russia begin to settle in the Great Plains states and provinces.

1880 For the next 40 years, large numbers of Russians emigrate to North America.

1906 Molokans settle near Los Angeles.

1917 The Communist Revolution begins in Russia; the United States declares war on Germany and enters World War I.

1922 The Union of Soviet Socialist Republics (U.S.S.R.) is created.

1938 Vladimir Zworykin's research leads to the development of television.

1939 Igor Sikorsky invents the helicopter.

1951 The last World War II refugees from the Soviet Union immigrate to the United States.

1991 The Soviet Union collapses; Russia is again an independent nation.

1993 Russian president Boris Yeltsin meets with U.S. President Bill Clinton to discuss the relationship between the two countries.

1995 The province of Chechnya attempts to break away from Russia, resulting in a two-year-long armed conflict.

1998 A financial crisis rocks Russia and leads to political upheaval.

2000 Vladimir Putin is elected president of Russia.

2001 U.S. President George W. Bush meets with Russia's President Putin to discuss actions the two countries will take against terrorists in Afghanistan and around the world. Bush also indicates that the United States will pull out of the anti-ballistic missile treaty signed with Russia in 1972.

2002 The Russian American population is estimated at more than 11 million.

2006 According to the American Community Survey, a project of the U.S. Census Bureau, there are 3.1 million Russian Americans living in the United States.

Glossary

Asylum the protection given by one country to refugees from another country.

Autocrat a person ruling with unlimited authority.

Cold War the hostility and sharp conflict in economics, diplomacy, and so on, between the United States and the former Soviet Union, without actual warfare, during the 1960s and 1970s.

Communist someone who believes that the wealth of a nation can be shared equally by all of its citizens.

Concentration camp a prison camp used to hold citizens or political prisoners.

Czar an emperor (also spelled tsar).

Emigrant a person who moves away from his or her country to settle in another country.

Genocide a systematic program to destroy an entire ethnic group of people.

Herring a North Atlantic fish often preserved by being smoked, salted, or canned.

Immigrant a person who comes to live in a new country or region.

Inferiority complex a feeling that one is below the same level as other people.

Influx a continual arrival of people.

Lodger a roomer or boarder in an apartment house.

Mennonites a religious sect founded in Switzerland in the 16th century that opposes the taking of oaths, infant baptism, and military service.

Molokans literally "milk drinkers" in Russian; this peace-loving group broke away from the Russian Orthodox church in the 18th century and was so named for drinking milk during the church's fast at Lent, which was unacceptable.

Oppression a feeling of being weighed down with worries or problems.

Pacifist a person who is opposed to the use of force under any circumstances.

Pale a region between the Black Sea and the Baltic Sea where Russian Jews were forced to live; short for the "Pale of Settlement."

Pogrom an organized, government-sanctioned persecution and massacre of a minority group.

Recruit to increase or retain the number of.

Self-sufficiency having the necessary resources to get along without help.

Serf a person who is bound to his or her master's land and transferred with it to a new owner.

Stratum a group in a society defined by birth, income, education, and so on.

Sweatshop a place where people work in a confined area for long periods of time for low wages; characterized by high heat, especially in summer.

Tyranny the cruel or unjust use of power or authority.

Visa a document that permits a person to travel in or pass through a country.

Famous Russian Americans

Mikhail Baryshnikov, ballet dancer

Saul Bellow, author

Irving Berlin, composer

Sergey Brin, cofounder of Google

Joseph Brodsky, poet

Milla Jovovich, model, actress, and fashion designer

Nastia Liukin, Olympic champion gymnast

Vladimir Nabokov, author

Ayn Rand, author

Olesya Rulin, actress

Maria Sharapova, professional tennis star

Igor Sikorsky, inventor of the helicopter

Issac Stern, musician

Igor Stravinsky, composer

Natalie Wood, actress

Vladimir Zworykin, scientist who invented the electron microscope and helped develop television

Further Reading

Coan, Peter M. *Ellis Island Interviews: In Their Own Words*. New York: Facts on File, 1997.

Lingen, Marissa. *The Jewish Americans*. Philadelphia: Mason Crest Publishers, 2003.

Ferry, Steven. *Cultures of America: Russian Americans*. Tarrytown: Benchmark Books, 1996.

Jacobs, Nancy R., Rein, Mei Ling, and Seigel, Mark S. eds., *Immigration and Illegal Aliens—Burden or Blessing?* Wylie: Information Plus, 1999.

Nugent, Walter. *Crossings: The Great Trans-Atlantic Migrations, 1870–1914*. Bloomington: Indiana University Press, 1992.

Wertsman, Vladimir. *The Russians in America: A Chronology and Fact Book*. Dobbs Ferry: Ocean Publications, Inc., 1977.

Tracing Your Russian American Ancestors

Carmack, Sharon DeBartolo. *A Genealogist's Guide to Discovering Your Immigrant and Ethnic Ancestors: How to Find and Record Your Unique Heritage*. Cincinnati: Betterway Books, 2000.

Glazier, Ira A. *Migration from the Russian Empire: Lists of Passengers Arriving at the Port of New York, 1875–1910*. Wilmington, Del.: Scholarly Resources, 1995.

Schaefer, Christina K. *Instant Information on the Internet! A Genealogist's No-Frills Guide to the Fifty States and the District of Columbia*. Baltimore: Genealogical Publishing Co., 1999.

Internet Resources

http://www.census.gov

The official Web site of the U.S. Bureau of the Census contains information about the most recent census taken in 2000.

http://www12.statcan.ca/english/census/index.cfm

The Web site for Canada's Bureau of Statistics, which includes population information updated for the most recent census.

http://www.ellisisland.org/

This Web site is devoted to the history of Ellis Island and the immigrants who came through its doors.

http://www.russianamericanculture.com/

The official Web site of the Russian American Cultural Center, which seeks to integrate Russian immigrants into the American lifestyle while educating the public about Russian culture, history and art.

http://www.russian-americans.org/

The official Web site of the Congress of Russian Americans, a non-profit organization that preserves the spiritual and cultural heritage of Russian Americans.

http://www.rach-c.org/

The Russian American Cultural Heritage Center is a non-profit group that works with immigrants to help them assimilate into American culture while still keeping Russian traditions alive.

Index

Photo Credits

Contributors

Barry Moreno has been librarian and historian at the Ellis Island Immigration Museum and the Statue of Liberty National Monument since 1988. He is the author of *The Statue of Liberty Encyclopedia*, which was published by Simon & Schuster in October 2000. He is a native of Los Angeles, California. After graduation from California State University at Los Angeles, where he earned a degree in history, he joined the National Park Service as a seasonal park ranger at the Statue of Liberty; he eventually became the monument's librarian. In his spare time, Barry enjoys reading, writing, and studying foreign languages and grammar. His biography has been included in *Who's Who Among Hispanic Americans*, *The Directory of National Park Service Historians*, *Who's Who in America*, and *The Directory of American Scholars*.

Richard A. Bowen is a Wisconsin author whose books include *The Art of Hearing: Seven Practical Methods for Improving Your Hearing*, *Meeting Your Match—His Story*, and *Spirit and Nature*, a book of verse. He is co-owner of Ariadne Publishers and editor of the "Spiritual Awakenings" quarterly.